TEACHING TR

EARLY LEARNING ON SHORT DAY T

Written and Compiled by Elizabeth McKinn
Illustrated by Susan Dahlman

Warren Publishing House
Everett, Washington

We wish to thank the following teachers, childcare workers, and parents for contributing some of the activities in this book: Cathryn Abraham, St. Charles, IL; Julie Bakerlis, Dudley, MA; Sr. Mary Bezold, Corbin, KY; Reva Bucholtz, Tucson, AZ; Ann Champeau, Norman, OK; Neoma Kreuter, El Dorado Springs, CO; Kathy McCullough, St. Charles, IL; Sharon Olson, Minot, ND; Susan M. Paprocki, Northbrook, IL; Dawn Picolelli, Wilmington, DE; Debbie Scofield, Niceville, FL; Betty Silkunas, Lansdale, PA; Jacki Smallwood, Royersford, PA; Diane Thom, Maple Valley, WA; Bobbie Lee Wagman, Milton, WI; Kristine Wagoner, Puyallup, WA.

Editorial Staff
Managing Editor: Kathleen Cubley
Contributing Editors: Gayle Bittinger, Kate Ffolliott, Susan Hodges, Jean Warren
Copy Editor: Mae Rhodes
Proofreader: Kris Fulsaas
Editorial Assistant: Kate Ffolliott

Design and Production Staff
Art Manager: Jill Lustig
Book Design: Lynne Faulk
Layout Production: Sarah Ness
Cover Design: Brenda Mann Harrison
Cover Illustration: Susan Dahlman
Production Manager: JoAnna Brock

ISBN 157029-070-9

Library of Congress Catalog Number 95-60513
Printed in the United States of America
Published by: Warren Publishing House
P.O. Box 2250
Everett, WA 98203

20 19 18 17 16 15 14 13 12 11 10 9 8 7 6 5 4 3 2 1

INTRODUCTION

Whether you are viewing exhibits at the museum or camping out in the woods, you can turn short trips into teaching trips just by making use of the surroundings and ordinary items found at the site.

You already know that going on a short trip can be a learning experience in itself, but why not enrich the experience for both you and your child? With *Teaching Trips* at your side, you can instantly provide your child with fun, educational ideas wherever you are.

To make the most of your short trips, plan to include one or two of the activities from *Teaching Trips* each time you travel. You and your child will enjoy doing such things as recording animal sounds at the zoo, looking for planes painted in matching colors at the airport, or lining up and counting shells at the beach.

Teaching Trips is divided into eleven chapters: Museum, Zoo, Park, Airport, Circus, Picnic, Farm, Woods, Beach, Travel Games, and Trip Tips.

Each of the first nine chapters contains fun, easy activities to do at the trip site, followed by related activities that you and your child can do when you return home. A chapter of travel games provides a variety of activities to do in the car or at the site. And a final chapter offers helpful hints for making any outing with young children run smoothly.

The activities in the chapters are grouped into the areas of language, creativity, thinking skills, coordination, science, and self-awareness. At first glance, these activities might seem to be "just play." However, as the introductory sentences to the activities explain, each utilizes a specific skill—one that forms part of a foundation necessary for higher learning.

For instance, participating in dramatic-play and oral-language activities prepares your child for communicating clearly with others. Art projects spark the imagination needed for effective reading, writing, and scientific speculation. Playing matching and sorting games develops an understanding of likes and differences, a skill used in nearly all learning areas, including math, science, reading, and writing.

Also, small-muscle coordination activities pave the way for learning how to use a pen or pencil, science activities promote thinking skills, and self-esteem activities lead to building self-confidence, so necessary for your child's success in all learning areas.

Since you are your child's first teacher, use the opportunity of short trips to start teaching him or her basic skills and concepts. Just open to a page for one of the trips you plan to take today, skim through the easy step-by-step instructions, and begin!

A WORD ABOUT SAFETY

All the activities in *Teaching Trips* are appropriate for the ages listed. However, keep in mind that when doing the activities, an adult should supervise to make sure that children do not put materials or objects into their mouth.

As for art materials, such as scissors, glue, or felt tip markers, use those that are specifically labeled as safe for children unless the materials are to be used only by an adult.

CONTENTS

MUSEUM CHECKLIST

This prereading-prewriting activity provides a fun plan for your museum visit.

MUSEUM

—

AGES
3 to 5

YOU WILL TEACH
Language

YOU WILL NEED
pen
paper
museum paintings or
exhibits

— 8 —

1) Before going to the museum, talk with your child about the kinds of things you will see there.

2) With your child, make a picture list of five to eight items to look for. If an art museum is your destination, the list might include pictures of such things as a boat, a tree, a boy, and a girl. For a science museum, you might include a giant dinosaur and a butterfly exhibit on your list.

3) When you get to the museum, give your child the list and a pen.

4) Help your child check off the items on the list that you see as you walk through the museum.

TELL THE STORY

Help develop your child's imagination with this storytelling activity.

1) As you walk through the museum, look for a painting or exhibit that seems especially interesting to your child.

2) Ask your child if the painting or exhibit tells a story and if so, encourage him or her to tell it to you.

3) As your child tells the story, lead him or her to include details about what happened before and what will happen in the future.

4) Let your child choose a painting or exhibit for you to tell a story about.

MUSEUM

—

AGES
3 to 5

—

YOU WILL TEACH
Language

—

YOU WILL NEED
museum painting or exhibit

WHAT IF?

This oral-language activity uses thinking skills.

MUSEUM

AGES
4 to 5

YOU WILL TEACH
Language

YOU WILL NEED
museum painting or exhibit

1) Choose a painting or exhibit at the museum.

2) Ask your child a question such as, "What if you were on that boat in the water?" or, "What if that dinosaur could talk?"

3) Encourage your child to use his or her imagination when answering.

4) Let your child find a painting or exhibit and ask you a "What If?" question about it.

5) Continue the activity as long as you like.

POSTCARD MATCH

Use this matching activity to add something extra to your museum visit.

1) When you first arrive at the museum, visit the gift shop.

2) With your child, choose several postcards that have pictures of items that are on display at the museum.

3) Purchase the cards and give them to your child.

4) As you walk through the museum, have your child look for the items that are pictured on the postcards.

ANOTHER IDEA: *For a problem-solving activity to do at home, cut each postcard into several interlocking pieces and let your child put the postcard puzzles back together.*

11

VIEWING ART

Encourage your child's appreciation of art with this observation activity.

MUSEUM

AGES
3 to 5

YOU WILL TEACH
Thinking Skills

YOU WILL NEED
museum paintings

1) When you are viewing a painting with your child, ask questions such as the following.

- "What colors do you see in the painting?"

- "Can you see straight lines? Curved lines? Zigzag lines?"

- "Can you find circles in the painting? Squares? Triangles?"

- "If you could touch one thing in the painting, what would it be? How would it feel?"

- "How does the painting make you feel?"

2) Continue with similar questions when viewing other paintings.

STATUE

This whole-body movement activity will encourage your child's interest and delight in what he or she sees at the museum.

1) When there are few people around, stop with your child in front of a statue or painting of a person or an exhibit of an animal.

2) Talk about how the person or animal is standing, sitting, or lying down.

3) Ask your child to assume the same pose and remain still like a statue for a few seconds.

4) Continue in the same manner with other paintings or exhibits.

MUSEUM

AGES
3 to 5

YOU WILL TEACH
Coordination

YOU WILL NEED
museum statues, paintings, or exhibits

TOUR GUIDE

Try this dramatic-play activity after your child has experienced a guided museum tour.

**MUSEUM
AT-HOME FUN**

AGES
3 to 5

YOU WILL TEACH
Language

YOU WILL NEED
home environment

1) Talk with your child about how a museum guide leads a group around and talks about what is on display.

2) Let your child pretend to be a guide and take you on a "tour" of your home.

3) Demonstrate by taking your child to the kitchen and saying something such as: "This is the kitchen. We make dinner here. We keep pots and pans in this cupboard and foods like milk and eggs in the refrigerator."

4) Have your child continue in the same manner.

ART EXHIBIT

You and your child can enjoy creating art together with this activity.

1) After a visit to an art museum, encourage your child to create art of his or her own.

2) If possible, provide art materials that are related to the kind of art you have just seen, such as watercolors, collage materials, or clay.

3) Join your child in using the materials to create paintings or sculptures.

4) Display your finished paintings on a wall and your sculptures on a table for family and friends to admire.

ANIMAL DIORAMA

Try this craft activity after your child has seen an animal exhibit at a science museum.

**MUSEUM
AT-HOME FUN**

AGES
3 to 5

YOU WILL TEACH
Creativity

YOU WILL NEED
*shoebox
felt tip markers
brush
glue
dirt
leafy twigs
rocks
small plastic animals*

1) Place a shoebox on its side to use as a display case.

2) Let your child use felt tip markers to color the walls of the case as he or she wishes.

3) Have your child brush glue on the floor of the case and sprinkle on some dirt.

4) Help your child arrange leafy twigs and rocks inside the case to represent trees and boulders.

5) Let your child place small plastic dinosaurs or other animals in the case to complete the exhibit.

MAKING COLLECTIONS

This classification activity becomes meaningful after your child has made several museum visits.

1) Talk with your child about different collections you have seen at a museum.

2) Encourage your child to make collections of such items as rocks, spoons, shoes, or buttons.

3) Help your child exhibit his or her collections on shelves or in open boxes.

4) Use index cards and a pen to print labels for the collections as your child dictates.

5) Encourage your child to change his or her collection exhibits every now and then.

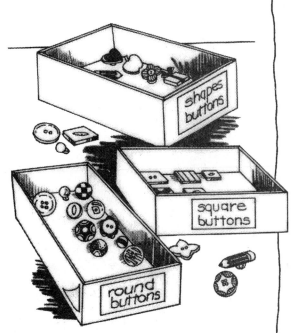

MUSEUM AT-HOME FUN

AGES
3 to 5

YOU WILL TEACH
Thinking Skills

YOU WILL NEED
collectible items
shelves or boxes
index cards
pen

WHAT'S AT THE ZOO?

This activity uses prereading and prewriting skills.

ZOO

AGES
3 to 5

YOU WILL TEACH
Language

YOU WILL NEED
zoo picture books
pen
paper

1) Before you visit the zoo, check out several zoo picture books from the library.

2) Read the books with your child, helping him or her to learn the names of such animals as giraffes, hippos, camels, and flamingos.

3) With your child, make a picture list of three or four animals he or she would like best to see at the zoo.

4) On your zoo visit, give the list to your child and help him or her check off the animals as you see them.

ANOTHER IDEA: *Let your child dictate questions he or she would like to ask a zookeeper. Take the questions with you when you and your child visit the zoo.*

FOLLOW THE MAP

Try this easy prereading activity when you have no set plan for exploring the zoo.

1) Pick up a copy of the zoo map at the ticket window.

2) Show the map to your child and point out various animal areas.

3) Let your child close his or her eyes and point to a spot on the map.

4) When your child opens his or her eyes, follow the map to the area he or she pointed to.

ANOTHER IDEA: *Take the map home and use it with your child to plot out future visits to the zoo.*

ZOO

AGES
3 to 5

YOU WILL TEACH
Language

YOU WILL NEED
zoo map

ZOO STORY

Using prereading and prewriting skills is the focus of this activity.

1) Take along a camera when you visit the zoo.

2) Snap a photo of your child's favorite zoo animal.

3) Later, when the photo has been developed, glue it to a piece of construction paper.

4) Have your child dictate a story about the animal as you write his or her words below the photo.

5) Slip the story inside a clear-plastic page protector and give it to your child to "read" back to you.

ANOTHER IDEA: *Do this activity each time you visit the zoo. Then fasten all your child's stories together to make a book.*

Elephants are big.

ANIMAL SOUNDS

This activity is a great way to reinforce listening skills.

1) Find a small portable tape recorder.

2) Carry the tape recorder with you when you visit the zoo.

3) As you walk by various animals, record the sounds they make.

4) Later, play back the tape and see if your child can identify each animal by its sound.

HINT: *You may wish to write down the names of the animals in the order in which you record them to use as a guide while listening to the tape.*

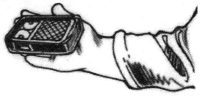

ZOO

AGES
3 to 5

YOU WILL TEACH
Language

YOU WILL NEED
audio tape
tape recorder
zoo animals

ZOO LUNCH

This prereading-prewriting activity helps develop creative skills.

ZOO

—

AGES
3 to 5

—

YOU WILL TEACH
Language

—

YOU WILL NEED
pen
paper
crayons (optional)
lunch foods
paper lunch bags

1) At home, make a menu with your child for a picnic lunch to take and eat at the zoo.

2) A suggested menu might include "Elephant's Choice Sandwich" (peanut butter sandwich), "Zoo Critters" (animal crackers), "Monkey's Best Dessert" (banana), and "Tropical Bird Nectar" (fruit punch).

3) Have your child use crayons to decorate the menu, if he or she wishes.

4) Let your child help make Zoo Lunches for both of you and pack them in paper lunch bags.

5) Take your lunches and the menu with you when you visit the zoo. Encourage your child to "read" the menu to you as you snack on the different foods.

UP-CLOSE LOOK

This observation activity adds something a little extra to a zoo visit.

1) Take a small pair of binoculars with you when you visit the zoo.

2) Show your child how to look through the binoculars to observe animals that are out in natural environments.

3) Also have your child use the binoculars when viewing animals that are up close, encouraging him or her to observe such details as the whiskers on a tiger or the colorful designs on a peacock's feathers.

4) Encourage your child to describe what he or she sees. What details are visible through the binoculars that are not visible with the naked eye?

ZOO

AGES
4 to 5

YOU WILL TEACH
Thinking Skills

YOU WILL NEED
binoculars
zoo animals

25

FUR, FEATHERS, SKIN

Your child learns classification skills with this activity.

ZOO

AGES
3 to 5

YOU WILL TEACH
Thinking Skills

YOU WILL NEED
notebook
pen
zoo animals

1) Take a notebook and pen with you when you visit the zoo.

2) Divide one of the notebook pages into three sections to make a chart.

3) Title the chart "Zoo Animals" and label the three sections "Fur," "Feathers," and "Skin."

4) As you and your child observe a zoo animal, talk about what its body covering looks like.

5) Ask your child to tell you under which heading the animal belongs and have him or her watch as you write its name on the chart.

6) Continue in the same manner with other animals you see.

7) Later, read the chart with your child as you talk about your trip to the zoo.

ANIMAL FAMILIES

This natural science activity uses classification skills.

1) At the zoo, choose a "family" of animals and visit several of its members. Here are some examples.

   - Cat Family—Tigers, panthers, lions
   - Ape Family—Monkeys, gorillas, chimpanzees
   - Bear Family—Black bears, brown bears, polar bears
   - Bird Family—Flamingos, parrots, peacocks
   - Reptile Family—Snakes, lizards, alligators

2) As you visit each animal in a family, talk with your child about how it is like the other family members.

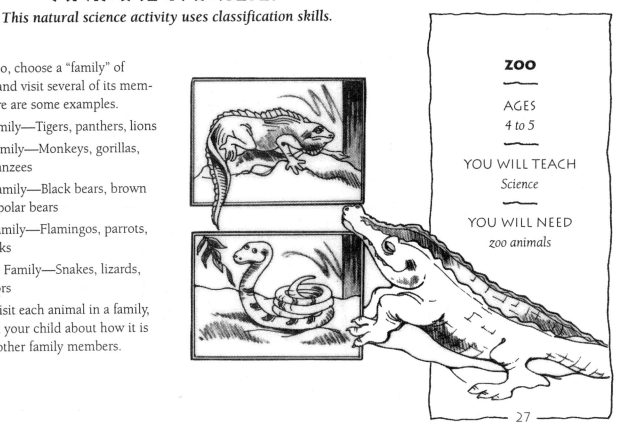

ZOO

—

AGES
4 to 5

—

YOU WILL TEACH
Science

—

YOU WILL NEED
zoo animals

PETTING ZOO

This sensory-awareness activity uses vocabulary-building skills.

1) At the zoo, take your child to the petting zoo section.

2) Talk with your child about the different animals on display. (Most petting zoos include such animals as a cow, a goat, a pig, a chicken, and a rabbit.)

3) Encourage your child to pet the animals and talk about how they feel to the touch. Use such words as *soft, silky, smooth, rough, bristly,* and *furry.*

4) Look around for other textures for your child to explore; for example, a rough fence post, a prickly hay bale, or a smooth-sided pail.

LET'S PLAY ZOO

This dramatic-play activity is sure to spark your child's imagination.

1) Let your child make a pretend zoo in one or more rooms of your home.

2) Help your child use such items as furniture and pillows to set up special areas for different stuffed animals.

3) Have your child pretend to be the zookeeper, doing such tasks as "feeding" the animals and giving them "baths" with an imaginary hose.

4) If any of the animals get "sick," encourage your child to take the role of veterinarian and "treat" them.

5) When the animals are all taken care of, let your child pretend to be a guide and take you on a tour of the zoo.

AGE VARIATION: *Help older children make a map of their pretend zoo.*

CLOTHESPIN ZOO

Your child is sure to have fun with this craft activity.

ZOO AT-HOME FUN

AGES
3 to 5

YOU WILL TEACH
Creativity

YOU WILL NEED
*pen
stiff paper
scissors
crayons or felt tip markers
spring-type clothespins*

30

1) Trace several four-legged zoo animal shapes onto stiff paper.

2) Cut out the animal shapes and trim off the legs.

3) Let your child use crayons or felt tip markers to color the shapes on both sides.

4) For each shape, give your child two spring-type clothespins.

5) Have your child color the clothespins with crayons or markers.

6) Show your child how to clip the clothespins to the animal shapes for legs.

7) Help your child display his or her Clothespin Zoo by standing the animals on a table or shelf.

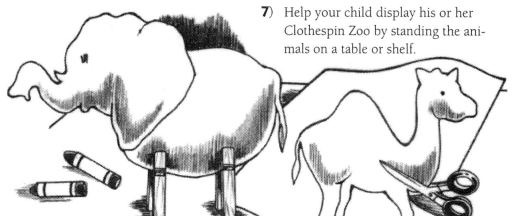

ANIMAL MASKS

Encourage dramatic play with this craft activity.

1) Give your child paper plates with eye holes cut out of them to use for making zoo animal masks.

2) For a zebra mask, have your child paint black stripes on the back of a paper plate. When the paint is dry, let your child glue on nose and ear shapes cut from construction paper.

3) For a leopard mask, have your child paint the back of a paper plate yellow. When the paint has dried, let him or her use a black felt tip marker to add spots. Give your child nose and ear shapes cut from construction paper to glue onto the plate for a face.

4) Glue a craft-stick handle to the back of each mask.

5) Let your child use the animal masks for dramatic play.

HINT: *To keep the paint from smearing, glue the ear shapes to the unpainted side of the mask.*

ZOO AT-HOME FUN

AGES
3 to 5

YOU WILL TEACH
Creativity

YOU WILL NEED
*paper plates
scissors
paintbrushes
black and yellow paint
glue
construction paper
black felt tip marker
craft sticks*

ZOO RIDDLES

You and your child are sure to enjoy this problem-solving activity.

ZOO AT-HOME FUN

AGES
3 to 5

YOU WILL TEACH
Thinking Skills

YOU WILL NEED
zoo picture book (optional)

32

1) Recite the following riddles. Have your child guess the names of the animals or point to their pictures in a book about the zoo.

- "I have a long tail. I live in trees. I like to eat bananas. Who am I?" (monkey)

- "I am gray. I have big ears. I have a long nose. Who am I?" (elephant)

- "I am king of the jungle. I have a golden mane. I like to roar. Who am I?" (lion)

- "I like to eat leaves. I have long legs. I have a very long neck. Who am I?" (giraffe)

- "I am white. I live where it is cold. I eat fish for my dinner. Who am I?" (polar bear)

2) Encourage your child to make up a simple Zoo Riddle for you to answer.

ZOO CHARADES

This problem-solving activity uses coordination skills.

1) With your child, look through a zoo picture book and talk about the different animals.

2) Invite your child to play a game of Zoo Charades.

3) Choose one of the animals, act out its movements, and ask your child to guess what animal it is.

4) Keep giving clues as necessary until your child guesses correctly.

5) Let your child choose a zoo animal and have you guess its name as he or she acts out its movements.

6) Continue taking turns playing the game as long as you wish.

ZOO AT-HOME FUN

AGES
2 to 5

YOU WILL TEACH
Thinking Skills

YOU WILL NEED
zoo picture book

33

NATURE WALK

This oral-language activity involves observation and listening skills.

PARK

—

AGES
2 to 5

—

YOU WILL TEACH
Language

—

YOU WILL NEED
park environment

36

1) Take your child to a park with a natural setting.

2) Walk slowly through the park, stopping frequently.

3) Encourage your child to examine the surrounding area and tell you what he or she sees.

4) Ask your child to close his or her eyes and listen carefully. What sounds can he or she hear?

ANOTHER IDEA: *Take along a tape recorder when you visit the park. Record sounds for your child to listen to and identify later.*

PLAYGROUND IMAGINING

Developing imagination is the focus of this dramatic-play activity.

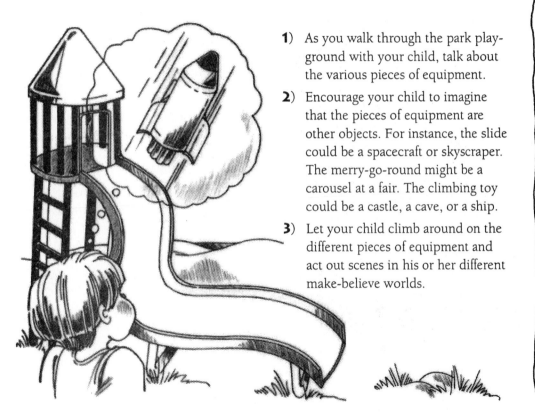

1) As you walk through the park playground with your child, talk about the various pieces of equipment.

2) Encourage your child to imagine that the pieces of equipment are other objects. For instance, the slide could be a spacecraft or skyscraper. The merry-go-round might be a carousel at a fair. The climbing toy could be a castle, a cave, or a ship.

3) Let your child climb around on the different pieces of equipment and act out scenes in his or her different make-believe worlds.

PARK

—

AGES
3 to 5

—

YOU WILL TEACH
Language

—

YOU WILL NEED
playground equipment

PARK RUBBINGS

Increase your child's awareness of textures with this art activity.

1) When you visit the park, take along some old, peeled crayons and pieces of thin paper.

2) As you walk with your child, look for items that have surfaces of different textures, such as tree trunks, stones, leaves, cement pathways, or metal grillwork.

3) Show your child how to make a rubbing by placing a piece of paper on a textured surface and coloring over it with the side of a crayon.

4) Encourage your child to make as many different rubbings as he or she wishes.

5) When you return home, display your child's rubbings and talk about the textures they reveal.

NATURE GRAPH

Your child will learn how to make a graph with this math activity.

1) Before going to the park, find a notebook and a pen.

2) Make a simple graph by drawing a grid on one of the notebook pages.

3) In each of the left-hand squares of the grid, draw a picture of something you might see at the park, such as a tree, a bird, an insect, a flower, or a small animal. Number the remaining squares across the top of the grid.

4) Take the notebook and pen with you when you go to the park.

5) Each time your child sees one of the things pictured on the graph, let him or her put a mark in a square following the picture.

6) When you return home, count the marked squares with your child and compare the totals of the various things he or she saw.

ANOTHER IDEA: *Let your child color in all the marked squares to make bars on the graph.*

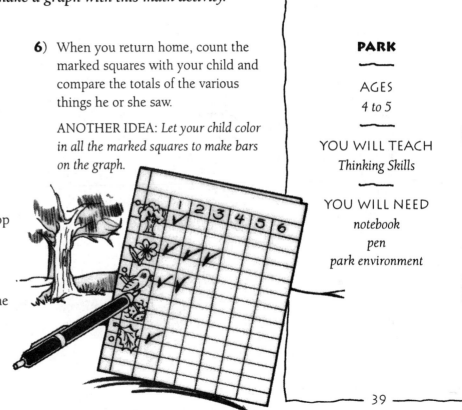

PARK

—

AGES
4 to 5

—

YOU WILL TEACH
Thinking Skills

—

YOU WILL NEED
notebook
pen
park environment

PARK COMPARISONS

This comparison activity involves observation skills.

1) As you walk through the park with your child, ask questions such as the following.

   • "Which tree is the tallest? Which is the shortest?"

   • "Which leaf is the largest? Which is the smallest?"

   • "Which rock is the heaviest? Which is the lightest?"

   • "Which tree trunk is the smoothest? Which is the roughest?"

   • "Which spot feels the coolest? Which feels the warmest?"

2) Encourage your child to ask comparison questions for you to answer.

SLIDE GAME

This simple experiment promotes predicting skills.

1) Take your child to the park playground.

2) Explain to your child that you are going to do a little experiment on the slide.

3) Show your child several items you have on hand, such as a ball, a pen, a rock, and a mitten.

4) Ask your child to predict which items will move down the slide the fastest and which will move down the slowest.

5) Have your child send the items down the slide and compare the results with his or her predictions.

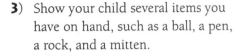

PARK

—

AGES
3 to 5

—

YOU WILL TEACH
Thinking Skills

—

YOU WILL NEED
*items on hand
playground slide*

SWING AND COUNT

This easy math activity provides fun for your child.

PARK

—

AGES
2 to 5

—

YOU WILL TEACH
Thinking Skills

—

YOU WILL NEED
playground swing

42

1) Find an empty swing for your child in the park playground.

2) When your child is seated in the swing, ask him or her to choose a number.

3) Push your child in the swing that number of times as he or she counts along with you.

4) When the swing stops moving, start the game again, if you wish.

FOLLOW THE LEADER

Vocabulary building becomes part of this whole-body movement activity.

1) At the park playground, play Follow the Leader with your child.

2) Have your child walk behind you, imitating your movements as you walk among the pieces of playground equipment.

3) Call out the names of the equipment pieces as you walk by them and have your child repeat the names after you.

4) Make the game challenging for your child by finding new or unusual ways to move over, under, and through the equipment.

5) Let your child have a turn being the Leader.

PARK

AGES
2 TO 5

YOU WILL TEACH
Coordination

YOU WILL NEED
playground environment

MERRY-GO-ROUND WALK

You and your child will enjoy doing this whole-body movement activity.

1) Take your child to the park playground.
2) Sit opposite your child on the merry-go-round with your feet on the ground.
3) Ask your child to slowly "walk" the merry-go-round around in a circle with you.
4) Then ask your child to help you walk the merry-go-round quickly, with one foot, with the other foot, and so forth.
5) Encourage your child to think of other ways for you to walk the merry-go-round together.

NATURE COLLECTION

A park is a perfect place to find items for this natural science activity.

1) Give your child a paper bag to take along when you visit the park.

2) Let your child search for different nature items, such as seeds, leaves, pine cones, rocks, and bird feathers.

3) Have your child put the nature items he or she finds into the paper bag.

4) When you return home, help your child group the items by kind on a large piece of cardboard.

5) Below each group, write a simple label, such as "Seeds" or "Feathers."

6) Let your child add to his or her Nature Collection whenever he or she wishes.

ANOTHER IDEA: *For a different kind of collecting activity, fasten a strip of masking tape sticky-side out around your child's wrist. Let your child attach small nature items he or she finds to the "bracelet."*

PARK

AGES
3 to 5

YOU WILL TEACH
Science

YOU WILL NEED
*paper bag
nature items
large cardboard
pen*

TOUCH WALK

This sensory-awareness activity can be done almost anywhere.

PARK

AGES
4 to 5

YOU WILL TEACH
Self-Awareness

YOU WILL NEED
playground environment

1) Take your child to the playground area of the park.

2) Have your child close his or her eyes as you lead him or her around the playground.

3) Help your child touch various surfaces, such as playground equipment, grass, and tree trunks.

4) Each time your child touches a surface, have him or her guess what it is and then open his or her eyes to see if the guess was correct.

LET'S PLAY PARK

Your child is sure to have fun with this dramatic-play activity.

1) Let your child make a play park for small plastic people and animals.

2) Give your child a large green bath towel or piece of green fabric to arrange on the floor for a base.

3) Let your child make trees for the park by standing twigs in balls of modeling clay.

4) For a pond, have your child use a crayon to color a paper plate blue.

5) Encourage your child to add other items such as rocks or wood block "buildings."

6) Let your child act out scenes in his or her play park with the toy people and animals.

ANOTHER IDEA: *With your child, make a pretend playground for stuffed animals that includes such things as a baking sheet slide, a scarf swing, a bookshelf climber, and a pan lid merry-go-round.*

NATURE COLLAGE

This art activity provides a way to make use of extra nature items your child has collected at the park.

AGES
3 to 5

YOU WILL TEACH
Creativity

YOU WILL NEED
*nature items
glue
plastic-foam food tray*

1) Set out small nature items and a bottle of glue.

2) Give your child a plastic-foam food tray that has been thoroughly washed and dried.

3) Let your child squeeze small amounts of glue onto the tray and place the nature items on top of the glue.

4) Encourage your child to continue until the entire tray is filled.

5) Let your child display his or her Nature Collage on a shelf or table.

IN THE PARK OR NOT?

Try doing this sorting activity after you and your child return from a park visit.

1) From magazines, cut pictures of people engaged in activities that might be done in a park, such as jogging, picnicking, playing on swings, wading in a pool, or observing birds.

2) Also cut out pictures of people engaged in activities that are not normally done in a park, such as vacuuming, baking cookies, brushing teeth, sleeping in a bed, or using a computer.

3) Mix up the pictures and place them in a pile.

4) Let your child sort the pictures into two groups: those that show activities people do in a park and those that show activities people do not do in a park.

HINT: *For a more durable game, cover the magazine pictures with clear self-stick paper.*

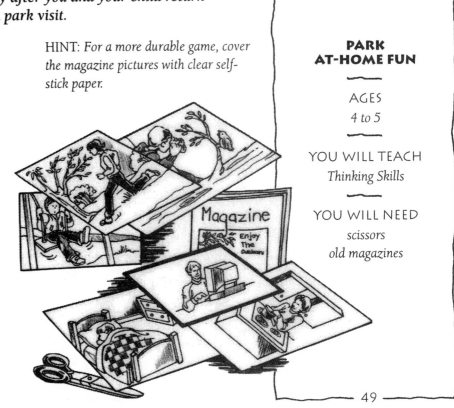

**PARK
AT-HOME FUN**

AGES
4 to 5

YOU WILL TEACH
Thinking Skills

YOU WILL NEED
*scissors
old magazines*

AIRPORT LEARNING

This prereading activity uses comparison skills.

AIRPORT

AGES
3 to 5

YOU WILL TEACH
Language

YOU WILL NEED
airport picture book
airport environment

1) Before your airport visit, find a picture book about airports.

2) Read the book to your child.

3) Use bookmarks to flag pictures that show several items to look for at the airport, such as the control tower, a jet plane, a person in uniform, and a cafeteria or snack bar.

4) Take the book with you when you and your child visit the airport.

5) As you come across each item that you flagged in the book, compare the item with the picture. Ask your child to tell you how they are alike and how they are different.

AIRPLANE STORY

Encourage your child to use his or her imagination when doing this storytelling activity.

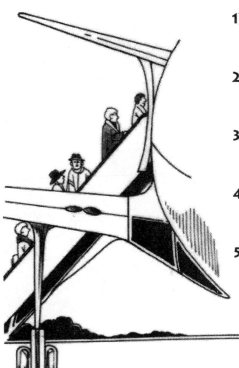

1) At the airport, stand with your child where you can see an airplane with passengers starting to board.

2) Begin telling a story about how the plane will fly up into the sky with all its passengers.

3) Ask your child to continue the story, telling what the passengers will do and see on their journey.

4) To end the story say, "When it's time to land, what will the plane do? Where will the passengers go?"

5) Encourage your child to choose a different airplane to make up a new story about.

AIRPORT

—

AGES
3 to 5

—

YOU WILL TEACH
Language

—

YOU WILL NEED
airplane and passengers

53

AIRPORT COUNTING

The airport provides many opportunities to try out this math activity.

AIRPORT

—

AGES
3 to 5

—

YOU WILL TEACH
Thinking Skills

—

YOU WILL NEED
airport environment

1) As you walk through the airport, count with your child such things as those below.

- number of people in uniforms
- number of bags on a cart or carousel
- number of airplanes on the tarmac
- number of gates in a sequence

2) Encourage your child to look for more things to count.

ANOTHER IDEA: *For a number-recognition game, name a number such as 3 and have your child search for it or listen for it over the loudspeaker.*

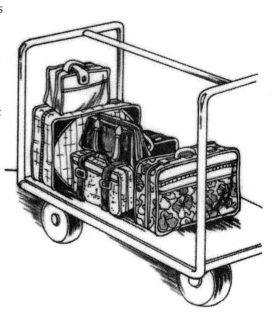

AIRPORT MATCHUPS

The airport provides many opportunities for using matching skills.

1) Stand with your child where you can see planes on the tarmac.

2) Talk with your child about how the planes are painted and what colors they are.

3) Ask your child to point to the matching-painted planes.

4) Continue by having your child look for other matchups, such as matching uniforms, matching-colored luggage, or matching kinds of foods displayed in a cafeteria or snack bar.

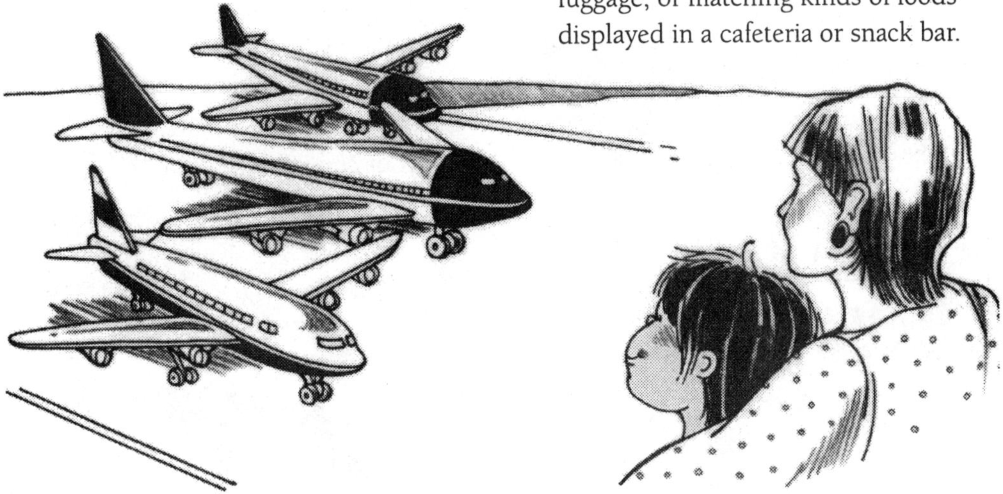

AIRPORT

—

AGES
3 to 5

—

YOU WILL TEACH
Thinking Skills

—

YOU WILL NEED
airport items

WHAT DO THEY DO?

*Your child will **enjoy this predicting** activity.*

AIRPORT

AGES
3 to 5

YOU WILL TEACH
Thinking Skills

YOU WILL NEED
airport environment

1) Stand with your child where you can see a plane that is being serviced on the tarmac.

2) Call attention to the different carts and trucks that go back and forth.

3) Ask your child to guess what each vehicle will do, such as carry baggage, deliver fuel, or deliver food.

4) Watch the action together and have your child check his or her responses.

MOVING AROUND

This whole-body movement activity is easy and fun to do.

1) Talk with your child about how big the airport is.

2) Together, look for "people movers" that help people get around the airport quickly and easily, such as escalators, elevators, moving sidewalks, and subways.

3) Let your child choose one or two of the "people movers" to take a ride on.

4) As you ride together, talk about safety rules and demonstrate how to follow them.

AIRPORT

AGES
3 to 5

YOU WILL TEACH
Coordination

YOU WILL NEED
airport environment

AIRPLANE RIDE

This dramatic-play activity uses matching skills.

**AIRPORT
AT-HOME FUN**

—

AGES
3 to 5

—

YOU WILL TEACH
Language

—

YOU WILL NEED
*chairs
pen
paper squares
tape
stuffed animals
magazines
plastic-foam food trays*

1) With your child, arrange chairs in rows to make an "airplane cabin."

2) Number paper squares in sequence and tape them to the chairs.

3) Write identical numbers on other paper squares to make "tickets" for stuffed-animal passengers.

4) While you play the role of pilot, let your child be the flight attendant and place the "passengers" in the matching-numbered seats.

5) When the plane "takes off," have the flight attendant do such things as hand out magazines to the passengers, serve them pretend snacks on plastic-foam food trays, and talk to them about the flight.

6) When the plane "lands," have the flight attendant help the passengers off the plane.

7) Trade places with your child and let him or her play the role of pilot.

ANOTHER IDEA: *Give your child a small suitcase and let him or her pack it for a pretend airplane ride.*

DOES IT FLY?

Using classification skills is the focus of this sorting activity.

1) From old magazines, cut pictures of things that fly, such as an airplane, a butterfly, a bird, a balloon, and a helicopter; and pictures of things that do not fly, such as a car, a boat, a dog, a wagon, and a fish.

2) Glue the pictures on pieces of construction paper.

3) When the glue has dried, mix up the pictures and give them to your child.

4) Have your child sort the pictures into two groups—things that fly and things that do not fly.

PLASTIC-FOAM PLANE

Flying this play airplane promotes large-muscle development.

1) On a plastic-foam food tray, draw an airplane body shape, a wings shape, and a tail shape as shown in the illustration.

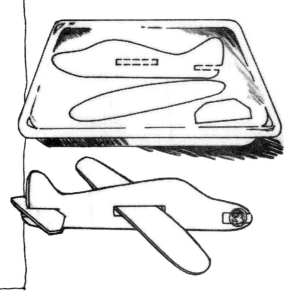

2) Cut out the shapes and make slits in the airplane body as indicated by the dotted lines.

3) Show your child how to insert the wings shape through the wide slit in the airplane body and the tail shape through the notched slit in the back.

4) Tape a penny to the nose section of the plane.

5) Let your child take the plane outdoors and have fun flying it in an open area.

ANOTHER IDEA: *For indoor play, let your child fly the plane around with his or her hand. You might wish to make a rule that when playing with toy airplanes, your child must be seated or kneeling.*

FLYING HIGH

This whole-body movement activity calls for using the imagination.

1) Take your child to an open area.

2) Ask your child to pretend that he or she is an airplane.

3) Have your child stand still, with arms outstretched for wings, until everything is "safe for takeoff."

4) Have the airplane pretend to take off, flying higher and higher until it is far above the clouds. What can it see as it looks down? Cars? Houses? Farms?

5) Finally, have the plane prepare to land, slowly flying lower and lower until it touches down on the ground.

AIRPORT AT-HOME FUN

AGES
3 to 5

YOU WILL TEACH
Coordination

YOU WILL NEED
open area

WHAT DO YOU HEAR?

Circus sounds become the focus of this listening activity.

CIRCUS

—

AGES
3 to 5

—

YOU WILL TEACH
Language

—

YOU WILL NEED
circus environment
pen
paper

1) At the circus, take turns with your child naming sounds you hear, such as an elephant trumpeting, a clown laughing, or the ringmaster announcing an act.

2) Make a list of the sounds as you name them.

3) When you return home, read the list with your child and have him or her try to reproduce the circus sounds from memory.

64

POSITION TALK

Try this vocabulary-building activity while watching various circus acts.

1) Talk with your child about spatial relationships as suggested in the following sentences.

   - The showgirl is riding *on* the elephant's back.
   - The clown is crawling *under* the car.
   - The tiger is leaping *through* the hoop.
   - The acrobats are high *above* the crowd, but the net *below* will catch them if they fall.

2) Encourage your child to describe similar circus scenes.

CIRCUS

—

AGES
3 to 5

—

YOU WILL TEACH
Language

—

YOU WILL NEED
circus acts

COLLAGE COLLECTION

Your child will enjoy remembering your circus visit with this art activity.

CIRCUS

AGES
2 to 5

YOU WILL TEACH
Creativity

YOU WILL NEED
small bag
circus mementos
glue or tape
cardboard

1) Take along a small bag when you go to the circus.

2) In the bag, have your child place circus mementos you collect, such as ticket stubs, circus programs, empty popcorn containers, and small souvenirs.

3) When you return home, help your child glue or tape the items to a piece of cardboard to make a circus collage.

4) Recall your time at the circus by talking with your child about the items in the collage.

CIRCUS COUNTING

Do this math activity at the circus whenever it seems appropriate.

1) With your child, count such things as those below.

   - number of steps you climb to your seats
   - number of children you see in a row
   - number of elephants in a parade
   - number of clowns in a ring
   - number of pairs of animals or people
   - number of acrobats in an act

2) Ask your child to select circus things for you to count together.

CIRCUS COLORS

Reinforcing color-recognition skills is the focus of this activity.

CIRCUS

———

AGES
3 to 5

———

YOU WILL TEACH
Thinking Skills

———

YOU WILL NEED
circus program
circus environment

1) Choose a color such as red.

2) Show your child a clown picture in a circus program and say, "I spy a red clown nose."

3) Have your child glance around the audience or circus arena for a matching-colored item and say something such as, "I spy a red coat," or "I spy a red ball."

4) Continue the game, taking turns naming other red items that you and your child see.

5) Choose a different color, such as blue, yellow, or green, and start a new game.

ANOTHER IDEA: *For a shape-recognition game, look for such items as circular rings, square cages, or triangular flags.*

LET ME BUY

This "grown-up" activity bolsters your child's self-esteem.

1) At the circus, make a picture list of snacks, such as popcorn, peanuts, or lemonade, that you want to purchase.

2) After each picture, write *X*'s to indicate how many of the snacks you need to buy for you, your child, and any friends or family members who are with you. (Eating popcorn or peanuts is not recommended for children under age 3.)

3) Go with your child to the concession area.

4) Help your child use the list to order the number of snacks needed and let him or her hand over the money for payment.

BE A CLOWN

Your child will have fun clowning around with this dramatic-play activity.

CIRCUS AT-HOME FUN

— · —

AGES
3 to 5

— · —

YOU WILL TEACH
Language

— · —

YOU WILL NEED
measuring cup
cornstarch
measuring spoons
water
cold cream
small containers
food coloring
old dress-up clothes

1) Make clown makeup by mixing together ⅓ cup cornstarch, 2 tablespoons plus 2 teaspoons water, and 2 tablespoons plus 2 teaspoons cold cream.

2) Divide the mixture into four small containers and add drops of food coloring as desired.

3) Apply the makeup to your child's face to create a clown face.

4) Let your child put on old dress-up clothes and perform clown acts for you.

5) Encourage your child to describe the clown acts as he or she performs.

PAPER PLATE CLOWN

Your child creates an original clown face with this art activity.

1) Give your child a paper plate for a clown face and a large triangle cut from construction paper for a hat.

2) Show your child how to glue the hat to the top part of the clown face.

3) Cut small circles, squares, and triangles out of construction paper.

4) Let your child glue the shapes on the clown face for facial features any way he or she wishes.

5) Give your child circle stickers or construction paper circles to attach to the clown hat for decorations. Provide a cotton ball for a pompom.

6) Let your child complete his or her clown by gluing pieces of curly gift-wrap ribbon "hair" to the sides of the plate.

7) Display the Paper Plate Clown on a wall or door, if your child wishes.

CIRCUS AT-HOME FUN

AGES
2 to 5

YOU WILL TEACH
Creativity

YOU WILL NEED
paper plate
scissors
construction paper
glue
circle stickers (optional)
cotton ball
curly gift-wrap ribbon

CIRCUS TRAIN

With this craft activity, your child helps make a toy that can be played with over and over again.

1) Select four or five cardboard boxes that are about the same size.

2) Arrange the boxes in a line on spread-out newspaper, open-sides up.

3) Let your child decorate the boxes by brushing on paint and gluing on colored paper scraps.

4) Hook the boxes together with heavy yarn and attach a yarn pull-handle.

5) Let your child place toy animals in the decorated Circus Train and pull them around the house.

ANOTHER IDEA: *Hook together empty Barnum's Animals animal cracker boxes to make a circus train. Let your child place a few small plastic animals or animal crackers inside the train cars.*

IN THE RING

Your child practices addition and subtraction with this math activity.

1) Use a long piece of yarn to make a "circus ring" on the floor.

2) Inside the ring, place six small plastic animals to represent circus animals.

3) Ask your child, "How many animals are in the ring?" and help him or her with the counting.

4) Move several of the animals outside the ring. Ask, "How many animals have left the ring?" then, "How many animals are still inside?"

5) Place several animals back in the ring and ask, "How many animals are in the ring now?"

6) Repeat the game, each time adding or subtracting a different number of animals.

CIRCUS PERFORMER MOVES

This whole-body movement activity is easy and fun to do.

**CIRCUS
AT-HOME FUN**

—

AGES
3 to 5

—

YOU WILL TEACH
Coordination

—

YOU WILL NEED
masking tape

74

1) Have your child pretend to be different circus performers such as the following.

- Tightrope Walker—Let your child walk very slowly, with arms outstretched for balance, along a strip of masking tape attached to the floor.

- Acrobat—Have your child do acrobatic tricks, such as forward and backward rolls, cartwheels, headstands, and splits.

- Clown—Let your child do clownlike capers such as running and toppling over, jumping, wiggling, pretending to trip over things, and making exaggerated motions of all kinds.

2) Encourage your child to choose other kinds of circus performers to imitate.

CIRCUS ANIMAL MOVES

You and your child are sure to enjoy this whole-body movement activity.

1) Take the role of ringmaster and announce each "act" as your child pretends to be circus animals such as the following.

   • Prancing Horse—Encourage your child to dance and prance around in a circle, pretending that a bareback rider is on his or her back.

   • Circus Elephant—Have your child bend over, clasp his or her hands together for a trunk, and stomp around in a circle, gently swinging the "trunk" from side to side.

   • Tiger Act—Hold a hoop upright as your child pretends to be a tiger stepping or jumping back and forth through it.

2) Can your child think of other circus animals to imitate?

FAMILY FAVORITES

Your child helps you plan a family picnic with this prereading-prewriting activity.

PICNIC

AGES
4 to 5

YOU WILL TEACH
Language

YOU WILL NEED
pen
paper

1) Before going on a picnic, let family members have a chance to contribute ideas.

2) With your child, make a list such as this: "Favorite Picnic Place, Favorite Picnic Food, Favorite Picnic Soft Drink, Favorite Picnic Activity, Favorite Friend to Invite."

3) Let your child ask each family member to name one or more "favorites" as you write the responses on the list.

4) Read through the completed list with your child.

5) Together, check off items on the list as you plan and prepare your family picnic.

PICNIC STORY BASKET

Try doing this storytelling activity while you are unpacking your picnic basket.

1) At the picnic site, invite your child to sit with you beside your picnic basket.

2) Start telling a picnic story and have your child take one item at a time out of the basket.

3) As your child does so, incorporate the items into your picnic story.

4) Continue the story until all the items have been removed from the basket.

ANOTHER IDEA: *Let your child help you make up another story as you put items back into the picnic basket to take home.*

PICNIC

—

AGES
2 to 5

—

YOU WILL TEACH
Language

—

YOU WILL NEED
*picnic basket
picnic items*

P PICNIC

Planning a picnic is the perfect time to try this letter-recognition activity.

1) Tell your child that you are going to have a *P Picnic*.

2) Together, tear out magazine pictures of foods with names that begin with *P*, such as peanut butter, pizza, popcorn, pretzels, pickles, peaches, pudding, and punch.

3) Let your child glue the pictures on paper to make a picture list.

4) Print the names of the foods next to the pictures and read over the list with your child.

5) Prepare a picnic lunch together, choosing from foods that are on your list.

6) Discuss the names of the *P* foods as you and your child enjoy your picnic.

COLOR PICNIC

Enjoy this color-recognition activity when just you and your child are going on a picnic.

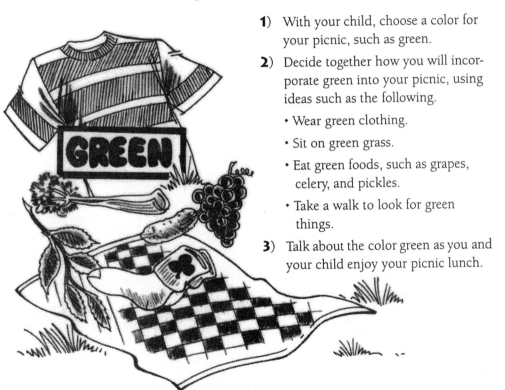

1) With your child, choose a color for your picnic, such as green.

2) Decide together how you will incorporate green into your picnic, using ideas such as the following.

   • Wear green clothing.

   • Sit on green grass.

   • Eat green foods, such as grapes, celery, and pickles.

   • Take a walk to look for green things.

3) Talk about the color green as you and your child enjoy your picnic lunch.

PICNIC

—

AGES
2 to 5

—

YOU WILL TEACH
Thinking Skills

—

YOU WILL NEED
green items and foods

WHAT'S INSIDE?

This activity uses problem-solving skills.

PICNIC

—

AGES
3 to 5

—

YOU WILL TEACH
Thinking Skills

—

YOU WILL NEED
*picnic basket
familiar objects*

— 82 —

1) Choose a time at your picnic when the picnic basket is empty.

2) Have your child close his or her eyes while you hide a familiar object inside the basket.

3) When your child opens his or her eyes, give clues about the object and have your child try to guess what it is. For instance, if you have hidden a ball say, "It is round. It bounces. You play with it."

4) Continue giving clues until your child names the object.

5) Hide another object in the basket and start the game again.

AGE VARIATION: *For younger children, set out several objects and name them* together *before hiding one of the objects in the basket.*

BEAR AT THE PICNIC

This memory game can be played with more than two people.

1) Set out several picnic items, such as a plastic spoon, a paper napkin, a mustard container, and a paper plate.

2) Talk about the items and help your child name them.

3) Have your child close his or her eyes and pretend to nap.

4) While your child is "asleep," pretend to be a bear who has come to the picnic. Snatch one of the picnic items and hide it.

5) Let your child open his or her eyes and guess which item is missing.

6) Continue until all the items have been taken.

AGE VARIATION: *Make the game more challenging for older children by setting out a larger number of items and moving them around each time your child closes his or her eyes.*

PICNIC

AGES
2 to 5

YOU WILL TEACH
Thinking Skills

YOU WILL NEED
picnic items

I'LL BE THE GROWNUP

Use this activity to boost your child's self-esteem.

PICNIC

AGES
3 to 5

YOU WILL TEACH
Self-Awareness

YOU WILL NEED
picnic items

1) Plan to have a picnic for two with your child.

2) Before you go, switch roles with your child, letting him or her pretend to be the parent while you play the part of the child.

3) Let your child decide such things as where to go for your picnic, what time to leave, what foods to take, and what games to play.

4) Have your child continue playing the role of parent while you enjoy your picnic together.

HINT: *Make clear ahead of time which decisions your child will be allowed to make when he or she is the parent.*

INDOOR BEACH PICNIC

This dramatic-play activity is especially fun to do in wintertime.

1) Spread out a blanket or tablecloth on the floor.

2) Add beach items, such as shells, a beach ball, or a beach umbrella, if you wish.

3) With your child, dress for the beach, putting on such items as bathing suits or shorts, sandals, and sunglasses.

4) As you sit on your "beach blanket," serve a picnic of summer foods, such as melon balls, frozen yogurt, and iced drinks.

5) After your picnic, encourage your child to act out pretend beach activities.

PICNIC AT-HOME FUN

AGES
2 to 5

YOU WILL TEACH
Language

YOU WILL NEED
blanket or tablecloth
beach items (optional)
beach clothing
summer foods

BASKET PICKUP

This activity teaches letter-recognition skills.

PICNIC
AT-HOME FUN

AGES
4 to 5

YOU WILL TEACH
Language

YOU WILL NEED
*picnic basket
pen
index card
tape
objects with names that
begin with* B
other objects

1) Place a picnic basket on the floor.

2) Print the letter *B* on an index card and tape it to the basket.

3) Set out several objects with names that begin with *B,* such as a ball, a box, and a book, and several objects that begin with other letters.

4) Print the beginning letters of the objects on separate index cards and tape the cards to the objects.

5) Name the objects with your child and have him or her put those with names that begin with *B* into the picnic basket.

ANOTHER IDEA: *Use other letters for this activity, such as P for picnic or L for lunch.*

PICNIC ART

Your child is sure to enjoy this art activity.

1) With your child, tear pictures of "picnic" foods from old magazines.

2) Have your child glue the pictures onto a paper plate to make a "picnic lunch."

3) For a tablecloth, give your child a large piece of paper, such as wrapping paper.

4) Let your child use a black ink pad to make fingerprint "ants" on the tablecloth.

5) Help your child glue or tape the paper plate to the tablecloth.

6) Let your child display his or her Picnic Art on a shelf or table.

PICNIC AT-HOME FUN

—

AGES
3 to 5

—

YOU WILL TEACH
Creativity

—

YOU WILL NEED
old magazines
glue
paper plate
large paper
ink pad
tape (optional)

FARM CHECKLIST

Use this prereading-prewriting activity to prepare your child for a visit to the farm.

FARM

AGES
3 to 5

YOU WILL TEACH
Language

YOU WILL NEED
pen
paper
farm items

1) Before going to the farm, make a picture list with your child of items to look for during your visit.

2) On your list, include such things as specific farm animals, an animal with a baby, an animal eating, a barn, a tractor, a pail, and a vegetable garden.

3) When you get to the farm, give your child the list and a pen.

4) As you walk through the farm, help your child check off items on the list that you see.

ACT IT OUT

This dramatic-play activity uses coordination skills.

1) As you walk around the farm, look for different tools and machines, such as shovels, rakes, pitchforks, pails, tractors, and trucks.

2) Point to a tool or machine and help your child name it.

3) Talk about how the tool or machine is used.

4) Have your child pretend to hold the tool or sit in the machine and act out how he or she would use it on the farm.

WHAT DID I SEE?

Your child is sure to enjoy this oral-language activity.

1) Take a notebook with you when you visit the farm.

2) On one of the pages, write a short story for your child such as the following: "One day I went to visit a farm. There were animals everywhere. The biggest animal I saw was a _____. The smallest animal I saw was a _____. The noisiest animals were the _____. The softest animals were the _____. The friendliest animals were the _____. If I could choose one animal to take home, I would choose the _____."

3) Later, read the story to your child and let him or her fill in the blanks as you write down his or her responses.

4) Let your child decorate the finished story with crayons or felt tip markers.

FARM CHART

This math activity involves classification skills.

1) Take along a notebook when you visit the farm.

2) On one of the notebook pages, make a chart titled "Farm Animals."

3) Have your child observe as you draw a line down the center of the chart to divide it into two sections.

4) Label one section "Two Legs" and the other section "Four Legs."

5) As you walk through the farm, have your child name animals you see and tell you whether they have two or four legs.

6) Write the animals' names on the chart in the appropriate sections.

7) When you return home, talk about the chart with your child and let him or her decorate it with felt tip markers.

ANOTHER IDEA: *Make charts to record such things as numbers of large and small pumpkins, numbers of animals sleeping and eating, or numbers of brown cows and black cows.*

FARM

—

AGES
3 to 5

—

YOU WILL TEACH
Thinking Skills

—

YOU WILL NEED
notebook
pen
farm animals
felt tip markers

LET'S COMPARE

Try this comparison activity whenever it seems appropriate.

FARM

AGES
3 to 5

YOU WILL TEACH
Thinking Skills

YOU WILL NEED
farm animals

1) As you walk through the farm, help your child become aware of differences by asking questions such as the following.

- "How is a pig's nose different from a cow's nose?"

- "How is a horse's tail different from a pig's tail?"

- "How are a chicken's feet different from a goose's feet?"

- "How is a barn different from a house?"

- "How is animal food different from people food?"

2) Encourage your child to talk about other differences he or she observes.

MY OWN FARM BOOK

Making your child the main character in a book increases his or her self-esteem.

1) When you visit the farm, take along a camera.

2) Snap pictures of your child in various places around the farm and with different animals.

3) Later, when the photographs have been developed, glue them in a blank book in an order that tells a story.

4) Write the story, using simple sentences, underneath the photos.

5) Read the book with your child, encouraging him or her to add more details as you look at the pictures.

6) Suggest that your child "read" his or her book to other members of the family.

FARM NURSERY RHYMES

This prereading activity reinforces rhyming skills.

**FARM
AT-HOME FUN**

AGES
3 to 5

YOU WILL TEACH
Language

YOU WILL NEED
*nursery rhyme book
large paper or posterboard
crayons or felt tip markers*

1) Find a book of nursery rhymes.

2) Select rhymes about the farm, such as "Baa, Baa, Black Sheep," "Little Boy Blue," "Hickety Pickety," and "Mary Had a Little Lamb."

3) Read the rhymes to your child and let him or her choose a favorite.

4) Print the rhyme on a large piece of paper or posterboard and let your child add decorations with crayons or felt tip markers.

5) Display the rhyme at your child's eye level.

6) Have your child "read" the rhyme with you as you move your finger under the printed lines.

LITTLE BOY BLUE

Little Boy Blue,
Come blow your horn!
The sheep's in the meadow,
The cows in the corn.
Where's the little boy
That looks after the sheep?
He's

NURSERY
RHYMES

FARM ANIMAL SOUNDS

This activity promotes listening and oral-language skills.

1) Find a farm animal picture book.

2) Look at the pictures with your child and talk about the sound each animal makes.

3) Make up a story about farm animals and tell it to your child.

4) Whenever your child hears the name of an animal, have him or her make that animal's sound.

ANOTHER IDEA: *For a different kind of farm animal sounds activity, sing "Old MacDonald Had a Farm" with your child.*

FARM AT-HOME FUN

—

AGES
2 to 5

—

YOU WILL TEACH
Language

—

YOU WILL NEED
farm animal picture book

MOTHERS AND BABIES

Vocabulary building is the focus of this language activity.

**FARM
AT-HOME FUN**

AGES
3 to 5

YOU WILL TEACH
Language

YOU WILL NEED
*farm animals and babies
picture book*

1) Check your local library for a picture book of farm animals and their babies.

2) Look through the book with your child.

3) As you do so, teach your child the names for farm animal babies such as these: cow–*calf*, sheep–*lamb*, pig–*piglet*, chicken–*chick*, horse–*colt*, duck–*duckling*, goat–*kid*, goose–*gosling*.

FARMYARD MURAL

You and your child will enjoy doing this art activity.

1) Lay a piece of large paper or cardboard on the floor.

2) On the paper, use felt tip markers to draw a simple farm scene that includes such things as a barn, a fence, and a tree.

3) With your child, look through old magazines and tear or cut out pictures of farm animals.

4) Let your child glue the animal pictures on the paper to complete the Farmyard Mural.

5) Display the mural on a wall for everyone to admire.

ANOTHER IDEA: *Draw a farmyard scene on a piece of construction paper. Let your child add farm animal stickers or stamp on farm animal pictures with rubber stamps.*

FARM AT-HOME FUN

AGES
2 to 5

YOU WILL TEACH
Creativity

YOU WILL NEED
*large paper or cardboard
felt tip markers
old magazines
scissors (optional)
glue*

FROM SEED TO PLANT

This sequencing activity helps your child learn about how vegetables grow.

1) Select four index cards.

2) On each card, draw a different stage of the growth of a carrot; for example, a seed in the ground, a sprouting seed, a small carrot growing in the ground, and a large carrot growing in the ground.

3) Mix up the cards and let your child arrange them in the proper order.

4) Follow the same procedure to make sequence cards for growing other familiar vegetables, such as corn or tomatoes.

ANOTHER IDEA: *For each group of sequence cards, make a fifth card that shows the vegetable on a plate, prepared for eating.*

GROWING SPROUTS

Your child grows a "crop" of sprouts, ready to eat in just days, with this natural science activity.

1) Find a small, shallow container, such as a disposable plastic food container or margarine tub.

2) Help your child place a flat layer of clean cotton in the bottom of the container and pour water over it until it is completely wet.

3) Let your child scatter cress seeds thickly all over the wet cotton.

4) During the next three to four days, have your child keep the cotton wet, observing as the seeds germinate and grow.

5) When the sprouts are about 1 inch tall, let your child "harvest" them for eating.

HINT: *Serve the sprouts in salads and sandwiches or sprinkle them over soups and vegetable dishes.*

FARM
AT-HOME FUN

—

AGES
3 to 5

—

YOU WILL TEACH
Science

—

YOU WILL NEED
shallow container
clean cotton
water
cress seeds

SMOKEY BEAR

Your child becomes aware of how to prevent forest fires with this prereading activity.

WOODS

—

AGES
3 to 5

YOU WILL TEACH
Language

—

YOU WILL NEED
Smokey Bear materials

1) Before going on a trip to the woods, talk with your child about the importance of being responsible with fire.

2) Contact your State Forester or regional office of the U.S. Forest Service to obtain a poster and other learning materials about Smokey Bear.

3) Use the materials to introduce your child to Smokey and his familiar message: "Only you can prevent forest fires."

4) Talk with your child about how Smokey teaches us that by preventing forest fires we are conserving trees, protecting animal homes, and preserving the woods for everyone to enjoy.

MINIATURE CAMPSITE

Your child uses rocks for "dolls" in this creative-play activity.

1) When you are camping, help your child collect nature items in the woods.

2) Let your child create a miniature campsite using the nature items; for example, a leaf could be used for a fire pit, twigs might be arranged as a tent, and moss could serve as a lake or stream.

3) Have your child select rocks to represent members of a family.

4) Let your child play with the rock people in his or her miniature campsite.

WOODS

—

AGES
3 to 5

—

YOU WILL TEACH
Creativity

—

YOU WILL NEED
nature items
rocks

NATURE SORT

Nature provides great materials to use for this sorting activity.

WOODS

—

AGES
2 to 5

—

YOU WILL TEACH
Thinking Skills

—

YOU WILL NEED
*bag or other container
nature items*

1) Carrying a bag or other container, take your child on a walk through the woods.

2) Together, collect nature items, such as leaves, pine cones, twigs, and stones, and place them in the bag.

3) When you return from your walk, let your child empty the bag and sort the items by kind into separate piles.

NATURE PATTERNS

Try using various kinds of nature items for this patterning activity.

1) Collect a number of small twigs and stones.

2) Clear a space on the ground for you and your child to sit.

3) In front of you, arrange several twigs and stones in a row in a pattern such as twig-stone-twig-stone.

4) Invite your child to use more twigs and stones to continue the pattern.

5) Repeat, arranging the items in various patterns for your child to continue.

6) Let your child create a pattern for you to repeat.

WOODS

—

AGES
3 to 5

—

YOU WILL TEACH
Thinking Skills

—

YOU WILL NEED
twigs
stones

WHAT SIZE?

This classification activity can also be done on a paper grid.

WOODS

—

AGES
3 to 5

—

YOU WILL TEACH
Thinking Skills

—

YOU WILL NEED
*small, medium, and large
nature items
stick
bare ground*

1) With your child, look for a small, a medium, and a large size of several different nature items, such as stones, pine cones, leaves, twigs, and moss pieces.

2) Using a stick, draw a grid on the ground that is three squares wide by several squares deep.

3) In the three top squares, place a small, a medium, and a large stone or other item.

4) Help your child sort the other nature items into small, medium, and large sizes and place them in the remaining squares of the grid.

CAMPING COMPARISONS

Try this comparison activity any time you are camping.

1) Ask your child to tell you how activities such as the ones below are done differently when camping than they are at home.

- cooking
- eating meals
- sleeping
- washing
- dressing
- playing

2) Which ways of doing things does your child like better? Why?

WOODS

—

AGES
3 to 5

—

YOU WILL TEACH
Thinking Skills

—

YOU WILL NEED
camping environment

IS IT LITTER?

This classification activity helps your child understand what litter is.

WOODS

AGES
3 to 5

YOU WILL TEACH
Thinking Skills

YOU WILL NEED
tray
litter items
nature items

1) When you are camping with your child, talk about the importance of keeping the woods free of litter.

2) On a tray, place several litter items, such as a plastic bag, an empty soft drink can, a scrap of paper, and a gum wrapper; and several nature items, such as a pine cone, a leaf, a feather, and a stone.

3) Explain to your child that litter is garbage that has not been put into a trash can.

4) Talk about the items on the tray and help your child divide them into two groups: litter items and nonlitter items.

5) Have your child throw the litter items into a trash can and place the nature items back on the ground.

ANOTHER IDEA: *Talk with your child about how litter left in the woods can be harmful to the animals who live there. For instance, the animals could get caught in plastic six-pack rings, get cut by rusted cans, or become sick from eating garbage.*

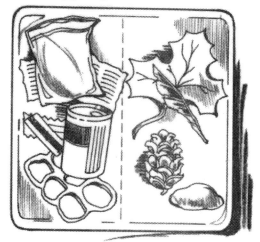

LEAVE IT THERE

This natural science activity teaches your child about ecology.

1) Explain to your child that when you come across a growing plant in the woods, you must remember this rule: Leave it where you find it.

2) Help your child understand that many of the plants produce seeds that lie in the ground until the following year when they will grow into plants that will produce the next year's seeds. If the plants are removed, there will be no seeds for the following year.

3) Take your child on a walk to practice the rule above.

4) Encourage your child to look at the plants you come across, but remind him or her that you must leave them where they are.

WOODS

AGES
3 to 5

YOU WILL TEACH
Science

YOU WILL NEED
woodland area with growing plants

TREE SAFARI

Help your child become more observant of trees with this natural science activity.

WOODS

———

AGES
3 to 5

———

YOU WILL TEACH
Science

———

YOU WILL NEED
variety of trees

1) Plan to take your child on a Tree Safari through the woods.

2) Before you go, explain that some trees grow leaves and are called deciduous trees, while others grow needles and are called evergreen trees, or conifers.

3) On your Tree Safari, whenever your child spots an interesting tree, have him or her try to answer questions such as: "Is the bark rough or smooth? Can you wrap your arms around the tree and tell me how wide it is? What color is the tree? Does it have leaves or needles? Would you say the tree is short or tall?"

4) When you return from your Tree Safari, ask your child to tell you what he or she learned about trees.

STREAM EXPLORATION

You never know what surprises might be in store when you try this natural science activity.

1) When you are going camping, take along a leg cut from an old pair of nylon pantyhose.

2) Poke two sticks in the ground on opposite banks of a narrow stream.

3) Using string, tie the top of the pantyhose leg to the sticks so that the opening is widened and the entire leg is floating in the water.

4) After about two hours, check to see what interesting items have been caught in the nylon "net" and talk about them with your child.

5) Put all the nature items that are caught back into the stream.

WOODS

—

AGES
3 to 5

—

YOU WILL TEACH
Science

—

YOU WILL NEED
leg from pantyhose
sticks
string
narrow stream

LET'S PLAY CAMP

Your child will have fun "camping" with this dramatic-play activity.

1) Create a campsite at home for your child to play in.

2) Set up a tent with a sleeping bag inside and put out several camp stools or chairs.

3) Move a small table to a spot near the tent and place camping cookware and eating utensils on it.

4) Help your child arrange rocks in a circle for a pretend fire pit.

5) Let your child play in the campsite, doing such things as cooking pretend meals, exploring the "woods" with a flashlight, and napping inside the tent.

CAMPSITE ART

This art activity can be done outdoors or inside.

1) Find a rectangular piece of thin cardboard.

2) Fold the cardboard in half and stand it upright to make a "tent."

3) Help your child collect a variety of nature items, such as pine needles, small pine cones, pebbles, feathers, and leaves.

4) Let your child decorate the sides of the cardboard tent by gluing on the nature items.

**WOODS
AT-HOME FUN**

—

AGES
3 to 5

—

YOU WILL TEACH
Creativity

—

YOU WILL NEED
*thin cardboard
nature items
glue*

WHEN I GO CAMPING

This memory game is always fun to play.

**WOODS
AT-HOME FUN**

—

AGES
3 to 5

—

YOU WILL TEACH
Thinking Skills

—

YOU WILL NEED
sticks

1) Arrange sticks in a pile to make a pretend campfire.

2) Sit by the "fire" with your child.

3) Take turns saying, "When I go camping, I always take my _____."

4) As each of you takes a turn, repeat all the items mentioned from the beginning of the game before adding a new item.

5) Continue playing as long as you wish.

AGE VARIATION: *For younger children, start the game over frequently so that the list of items does not become too long to remember.*

TRAIL SNACK

Making this portable snack helps promote small-muscle development.

1) Give your child a long piece of string with a large knot tied in one end and the other end taped to make a "needle."

2) Set out a bowl of *O*-shaped cereal pieces.

3) Let your child thread the cereal pieces onto the string.

4) When your child finishes, tie the ends of the string around his or her neck.

5) Let your child enjoy his or her necklace snack while exploring "trails" around a backyard campsite.

AGES
3 to 5

YOU WILL TEACH
Coordination

YOU WILL NEED
string
tape
O-shaped cereal pieces

SAND WRITING

Try doing this letter-recognition activity in dry or wet sand.

BEACH

—

AGES
4 to 5

YOU WILL TEACH
Language

—

YOU WILL NEED
sand
stick (optional)

1) At the beach, let your child help you find a smooth, sandy area.

2) Using a stick or a finger, write an alphabet letter in the sand.

3) Have your child trace over the letter while naming it.

4) Repeat with other alphabet letters.

SAND MOLDS

Your child will have fun with this creative-play activity.

1) When you go to the beach, take along a bag filled with sturdy containers, such as plastic measuring cups, plastic food tubs of various sizes, and small gelatin molds.

2) Let your child pack the containers full of wet sand, turn them over, and then remove the containers to reveal the molded sand shapes.

3) Encourage your child to create "cakes," a "house," or whatever else he or she chooses.

HINT: *Use a mesh bag, such as a citrus bag, to carry the containers. When you are ready to go home, just rinse the bag of containers with fresh water to wash away the sand.*

BEACH
—

AGES
2 to 5
—

YOU WILL TEACH
Creativity
—

YOU WILL NEED
bag
sturdy containers
wet sand

SHELL LINEUP

This ordering activity involves counting skills.

1) As you walk along the beach with your child, pick up different sizes of shells.

2) Have your child help smooth out an area in the sand.

3) Give the shells to your child and let him or her line them up on the sand from smallest to largest or from largest to smallest.

4) Count the number of shells with your child.

   ANOTHER IDEA: *Use small stones instead of shells.*

BEACH BLANKET FUN

Your child uses sensory clues in this predicting activity.

1) Spread out a blanket at the beach.

2) While your child closes his or her eyes, hide a familiar object, such as a ball or a sand shovel, under the blanket.

3) When your child opens his or her eyes, let him or her touch the object through the blanket and try to guess what it is.

4) After your child responds, have him or her look under the blanket to see if the guess was correct.

5) Let your child hide an object under the blanket and have you guess what it is.

BEACH

AGES
2 to 5

YOU WILL TEACH
Thinking Skills

YOU WILL NEED
blanket
familiar objects

SAND TOYS

Playing with these homemade toys encourages large-muscle development.

BEACH

AGES
2 to 5

YOU WILL TEACH
Coordination

YOU WILL NEED
plastic bleach bottle with cap
scissors
heavy cardboard
sand

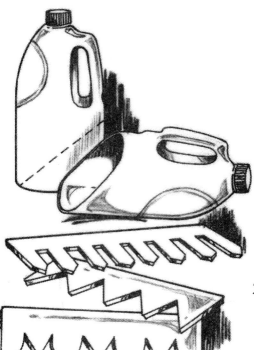

1) Before going to the beach, make the toys below.

   • Sand Scoop—Wash and dry an empty bleach bottle and screw the cap back on tightly. Cut off the bottom of the bottle diagonally to make a scoop with a handle.

   • Sand Combs—Cut heavy cardboard into rectangles about 6 by 12 inches. On one of the long sides of each rectangle, cut several notches, varying the shapes and sizes of the notches on each rectangle.

2) At the beach, let your child dig with the sand scoop and make patterns in the sand with the sand combs.

BURIED TREASURE

Digging for treasure encourages large-muscle development.

1) Find a pretty shell or rock on the beach.

2) Let your child help you make a large mound in the sand.

3) While your child closes his or her eyes, hide the shell or rock in the sand mound.

4) Have your child open his or her eyes and dig through the sand to find the "treasure."

5) Let your child bury the shell or rock in a mound of sand for you to find.

BEACH

—

AGES
3 to 5

—

YOU WILL TEACH
Coordination

—

YOU WILL NEED
*pretty shell or rock
sand*

FOLLOW THE TRAIL

Your child will enjoy this whole-body movement activity.

1) Find a smooth, sandy area at the beach.

2) With a stick, draw a long, straight line in the sand and have your child walk along it.

3) Continue drawing various kinds of lines for your child to follow—lines that curve, lines that zigzag, lines that stop and start, or lines that go round in circles.

4) Let your child use the stick to draw lines for you to follow.

UNDERWATER VIEWER

Your child uses observation skills with this natural science activity.

1) Before leaving home, make a viewer for your child to use at the beach.

2) Cut the middle section out of a large, plastic soft-drink bottle.

3) Cover one end of the section with plastic wrap and secure it with a large rubber band.

4) At the beach, show your child how to use the viewer to observe underwater scenes in a tide pool.

5) Stay with your child, encouraging him or her to describe what he or she sees through the viewer.

BEACH

AGES
4 to 5

YOU WILL TEACH
Science

YOU WILL NEED
sharp knife
plastic soft-drink bottle
plastic wrap
large rubber band
tide pool

COLLECTING JAR

This natural science activity helps make the decision of what to take home from the beach an easier one.

BEACH

—

AGES
2 to 5

—

YOU WILL TEACH
Science

—

YOU WILL NEED
plastic jar with lid
nonliving beach items
water
bleach

1) When you go to the beach, take along a plastic jar with a lid.

2) Give the jar to your child, explaining that he or she can take home any nonliving beach items, such as empty shells, rocks, or sticks, that will fit in the jar.

3) Encourage your child to take his or her time choosing just what he or she wants to keep.

4) When you return home, fill the remainder of the jar with water, add a few drops of bleach to keep the water fresh, and screw the lid on tightly.

5) Let your child display the jar on a table or shelf.

PUTTING ON SUNSCREEN

Applying sunscreen provides a perfect opportunity for trying this body-awareness activity.

1) When putting on sunscreen for the beach, talk with your child about why it is used.

2) Together, point to and name different body parts, such as arms, legs, and shoulders.

3) Rub sunscreen on parts of your child's body as he or she tells you where to apply it.

4) Ask your child to rub some sunscreen on you as you name different body parts.

5) Continue until both you and your child are completely protected.

BEACH

AGES
2 to 5

YOU WILL TEACH
Self-Awareness

YOU WILL NEED
sunscreen

BACKYARD BEACH

Try this dramatic-play activity on a warm summer day.

**BEACH
AT-HOME FUN**

—

AGES
3 to 5

—

YOU WILL TEACH
Language

—

YOU WILL NEED
*tub of sand
tub of water
shells
plastic fish
beach items*

1) Create a make-believe beach in your yard.

2) Set out one tub of sand and another of water.

3) Add some shells to the sand tub and a few plastic fish to the water tub.

4) Give your child beach items such as sand scoops and funnels, a string "fishing line," a large beach towel, sunglasses, a sun hat, and a small portable radio.

5) Let your child play at the pretend beach, doing such things as digging in the sand, "fishing" in the water, and relaxing in the sun.

FISH PUPPET

A fish puppet makes this storytelling activity fun to do.

1) Use a business-size envelope to make a fish puppet.

2) Tuck in the flap of the envelope.

3) Put your hand inside the envelope with your fingers at one end and your thumb at the other.

4) Indent the middle of the envelope toward your hand and fold your fingers and thumb together to make the puppet.

5) Use felt tip markers to draw on eyes, scales, and fins.

6) Open and close your hand to make the puppet "talk" as you tell your child a fish story.

BEACH AT-HOME FUN

—

AGES
3 to 5

—

YOU WILL TEACH
Language

—

YOU WILL NEED
business-size envelope
felt tip markers

BEACH PICTURE

Try doing this art activity after a trip to the beach.

1) Give your child a piece of blue construction paper.

2) Let your child brush glue across the bottom part of the paper and sprinkle on sand to make a "beach."

3) Have your child also glue on small shells or shell pieces, if you wish.

4) Cut a sun shape out of yellow construction paper.

5) Let your child glue the sun shape on the top part of the paper to complete the beach scene.

ANOTHER IDEA: *For a different kind of sand picture, let your child squeeze glue in designs onto construction paper and sprinkle on sand.*

MAKING WAVES

This homemade toy will provide your child with hours of creative fun.

1) Find a plastic jar with a lid.

2) Fill the jar two-thirds full of water.

3) Add several drops of blue food coloring and mix well.

4) Fill up the rest of the jar with mineral oil, getting rid of as many air bubbles as possible.

5) Secure the lid of the jar with strong glue.

6) Let your child hold the jar sideways and gently tip it back and forth to make "waves."

PICTURE THIS

Use this storytelling activity to stimulate your child's imagination.

TRAVEL GAMES

AGES
2 to 5

YOU WILL TEACH
Language

YOU WILL NEED
*scissors
old magazines
tape*

136

1) Cut interesting pictures out of old magazines.

2) When you are going on a trip in the car, tape one of the pictures where your child can see it while sitting in his or her car seat or seat belt.

3) Ask your child to describe the picture.

4) Together, make up a story about the picture, pausing often to let your child tell what happens next.

5) Keep a supply of pictures in your car and change them often on long trips.

MAP FUN

Your child is sure to enjoy this prereading activity.

1) Before going on a trip, draw a simple map that shows familiar landmarks you will be passing on your way.

2) When you get in the car, give your child the map and a pen.

3) Have your child use the pen to check off each landmark on the map as you pass it.

ANOTHER IDEA: *If your destination is a frequent one, cover the map with clear self-stick paper and let your child check off the familiar landmarks with a black crayon. At the end of the trip, just wipe off the crayon marks with a dry cloth and the map will be ready to use again.*

LOOKING FOR LETTERS

Reviewing the alphabet is the focus of this letter-recognition activity.

TRAVEL GAMES

AGES
4 to 5

YOU WILL TEACH
Language

YOU WILL NEED
road signs

1) As you are riding in the car, choose an alphabet letter such as *B*.

2) Point out one or two *B*'s you see in road signs.

3) Ask your child to look for more *B*'s as you are traveling.

4) To start a new game, choose another letter to search for.

5) Continue the game as long as interest lasts.

AGE VARIATION: *Ask older children to search for letters that spell their names.*

LULLABY
Baby
Boutique
25 Beacon Avenue
Next Exit

Branson

TRAVELING FLANNELBOARD

Your child is sure to enjoy this storytelling activity.

1) Get a new pizza box from a pizza restaurant.

2) Cut a piece of felt to fit inside the lid of the box and glue it in place.

3) From other colors of felt, cut out a variety of small shapes, such as circles, squares, triangles, flowers, hearts, cars, and bears.

4) Store the shapes inside the box.

5) To use the Traveling Flannelboard, let your child prop open the box lid and arrange the small shapes on the felt surface while making up stories about them.

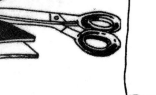

COOKIE TIN MAGNETBOARD

Magnets provide the fun in this creative-play activity.

TRAVEL GAMES

—

AGES
2 to 5

—

YOU WILL TEACH
Creativity

YOU WILL NEED
*cookie tin with lid
magnets*

1) Find a cookie tin with a lid.

2) Collect decorative kitchen magnets and place them inside the cookie tin.

3) Take the tin with you when you go on a trip.

4) Let your child use the cookie tin lid as a magnetboard, arranging and rearranging the magnets on it any way he or she wishes.

TRAVEL BOX

This travel toy can be stored in the car and used almost anywhere to promote creative play.

1) Find a plastic storage box, about 8 by 13 by 3 inches, with a lid.

2) Inside the box, store such items as a notepad, crayons, stickers, card games, and small plastic toys.

3) Let your child use the lid of the box as a "table" for drawing, playing games, or playing with toys.

TRAVEL GAMES

—

AGES
3 to 5

—

YOU WILL TEACH
Creativity

—

YOU WILL NEED
*plastic storage box with lid
notepad
crayons
stickers
card games
small plastic toys*

PAPER DOLLS

Magnets make this creative-play activity especially fun.

AGES
3 to 5

YOU WILL TEACH
Creativity

YOU WILL NEED
paper dolls
scissors
clear self-stick paper
glue
nonaluminum baking sheet
magnetic strip

1) Purchase a set of paper dolls.

2) Cut out the dolls, cover them with clear self-stick paper, and glue them, several inches apart, to an old non-aluminum baking sheet.

3) Cut out the doll clothes, snip off the tabs, and cover the clothes with clear self-stick paper.

4) Attach pieces of magnetic strip to the back of the clothes.

5) Let your child dress the paper dolls by placing the clothes on top of the dolls on the baking sheet. (The magnetic strip pieces will keep the clothes in place until your child wishes to change the dolls' outfits.)

QUIET GAME

Try this observation game when the noise level gets too high in your car.

1) Select an item that you are not likely to see often when traveling, such as a cement mixer or a yellow car with three people in it.

2) Ask your child to use only a "whisper voice" until he or she sees that item.

3) When the item is sighted, let your child resume talking in a normal voice.

4) To start a new game, choose another unfamiliar item and ask your child to look for it.

AGE VARIATION: *For younger children, choose a common item to make the game shorter, and for older children, choose a less common item to make the game longer.*

TRAVEL GAMES

—

AGES
3 to 5

—

YOU WILL TEACH
Thinking Skills

—

YOU WILL NEED
traveling environment

WHAT GOES WITH IT?

This classification game is fun to play in the car.

TRAVEL GAMES

AGES
3 to 5

YOU WILL TEACH
Thinking Skills

YOU WILL NEED
no materials needed

1) Name an item that usually is associated with another object and have your child name its partner.

2) Use examples such as these: salt–pepper, knife–fork, shoes–socks, soap–water, toothbrush–toothpaste.

3) Accept any answer that has an association of any kind.

BRAINTEASERS

This car game promotes problem-solving skills.

1) In a notebook, make short lists of Brainteasers for your child to respond to, such as the following.

- "How is a glove like your hand?"
- "Can you put your elbow in your ear?"
- "Can a cow really jump over the moon?"
- "Name one thing you can see in the sky at night."
- "Name one thing you can see in the sky in the morning."

2) Each time you go on a trip, select one of the Brainteaser lists, read the entries to your child, and have him or her respond.

NUMBER GAMES

These math games help make travel time pass more quickly.

1) When riding in the car with your child, try one or more of the following ideas.

   • Have your child look for a particular number, such as his or her age or the day's date.

   • Choose a number such as 3. On a short trip, see how many 3s you and your child can "collect" from road signs and license plates.

   • Mentally choose an object to count, such as motorcycles, busses, or red cars. Each time you see one of the objects, count out loud. Have your child try to guess what you are counting.

   • Select a category of items to count, such as supermarkets, vans, or billboards. With your child, see who can count the highest number of items in 10 minutes.

2) Let your child choose items he or she would like to count.

COLOR GAMES

These color-recognition games are great car activities.

1) With your child, try one or more of the following ideas.

- Call out a color name and type of vehicle such as, "Blue station wagon!" See which of you can spot the first one.

- Choose a color and take turns with your child naming things that are that color.

- Select a color you see inside the car and have your child name something outside the car that is the same color.

- Choose an item and have your child look for items that are the same color; for example, if you choose a pickle, have your child look for green items.

2) Encourage your child to think of other color games to play.

Red

TRAVEL GAMES

—

AGES
3 to 5

—

YOU WILL TEACH
Thinking Skills

—

YOU WILL NEED
traveling environment

147

TUBE LOOM

This weaving activity encourages small-muscle development.

TRAVEL GAMES

AGES
3 to 5

YOU WILL TEACH
Coordination

YOU WILL NEED
toilet tissue tube
scissors
yarn
ribbon (optional)
bag

148

1) Use a cardboard toilet tissue tube to make a loom.

2) Cut slits in both ends of the tube.

3) Run yarn lengthwise through the slits to create a warp as shown in the illustration.

4) Place the loom in a bag with additional pieces of yarn or pieces of ribbon.

5) When you are traveling, give the bag to your child and let him or her weave the yarn or ribbon pieces over and under the warp around the tube.

ANOTHER IDEA: *For a different kind of weaving activity, cut slits around the rim of a plastic lid and tape one end of a long piece of yarn to the back. Let your child weave the yarn across or around the lid, passing it through the slits any way he or she wishes.*

LACING CARD

Promoting small-muscle development is the focus of this activity.

1) Find a greeting card made out of stiff paper.

2) Cut off the front of the card, discarding the back.

3) Use a hole punch to punch holes about 1 inch apart around the edges of the card front.

4) Tie one end of a long piece of yarn through one of the holes.

5) Wrap the other end of the yarn piece with tape to make a "needle."

6) Give the card to your child and let him or her lace the yarn around it through the holes.

7) Unlace the yarn and let your child lace it around the card again.

TRAVEL GAMES

—

AGES
3 to 5

—

YOU WILL TEACH
Coordination

—

YOU WILL NEED
*greeting card
scissors
hole punch
yarn
tape*

BAG-O'-PLAYDOUGH

Let your child do this small-muscle development activity while traveling in the car.

TRAVEL GAMES

AGES
2 to 5

YOU WILL TEACH
Coordination

YOU WILL NEED
resealable plastic bags
playdough

1) Find two small, resealable plastic bags.

2) Place some playdough in one bag, press out the air, and seal the bag.

3) Put the bag of playdough into the second bag, press out the air, and seal it also.

4) Give the bag of playdough to your child to hold and squeeze in his or her hands.

MY SPECIAL BOX

Help make your child feel special with this self-esteem activity.

1) Before going on a trip, give your child a shoebox with a lid.

2) Let your child decorate the box with such things as felt tip marker designs, glued-on wrapping paper scraps, or stickers.

3) Help your child write his or her name on the box.

4) When traveling, let your child use his or her Special Box for keeping personal mementos he or she collects on the way.

5) Later, encourage your child to share the mementos, if he or she wishes.

TRAVEL GAMES

—

AGES
3 to 5

—

YOU WILL TEACH
Self-Awareness

—

YOU WILL NEED
shoebox with lid
felt tip markers
glue
wrapping paper scraps
stickers
travel mementos

BEFORE YOU GO

BEST TIME

Choose the best time to visit the site. For instance, go to a museum early in the day to avoid crowds. Visit the zoo at feeding time. Take your child to an ocean beach at low tide. Avoid an airport visit during the busy holiday season.

PLAN AHEAD

Familiarize yourself with the location ahead of time, if possible, and make sure that any tour you plan to take is appropriate. Keep in mind that young children enjoy seeing and touching things they can identify with and understand.

CALENDAR COUNTDOWN

To help your child figure out the number of days before your planned outing, first attach a sticker to the date of the outing on a calendar. Then starting with today's date, let your child mark off each day with a crayon and count to see how many days remain.

WHAT TO TAKE

MATCHING T-SHIRTS

If you are going to a place where there will be a lot of people, dress your child in a T-shirt that matches yours in color or design. That way, he or she can easily spot you in a crowd.

CAMERA AND TAPE RECORDER

Take a camera and a tape recorder (or a video camera) with you on outings. Later, you can use the photos and recorded tapes to review what your child experienced.

ON THE WAY

SNACKTIME

Pack snack foods, such as raisins, pretzels, small crackers, and fruit chunks, in sections of an empty egg carton. Your child can sample the snacks in the car or at the site.

SONG TAPES

Take tape recordings of favorite songs to play in the car. If your child gets restless, put on a tape and encourage him or her to sing along.

EMERGENCY BOX

For minor emergencies on outings, take along a box containing such things as facial tissues, small bandages, rubber bands, safety pins, and disposable wipes.

TAKE A BREAK

Before going on an outing, estimate the time it will take to get to the site. If it is more than half an hour, plan to take a break about halfway there.

ACTIVE TIME

Plan an active time before your visit if your child is expected to be quiet at the location. Schedule a restroom stop before arriving.

SCENIC ROUTE

If possible, take a scenic route when you go on an outing so that you can point out things of interest to your child along the way. This will help travel time pass more quickly.

AT THE SITE

LIMIT YOUR TIME

Don't spend too much time at the location. A half hour to one hour is usually long enough for young children.

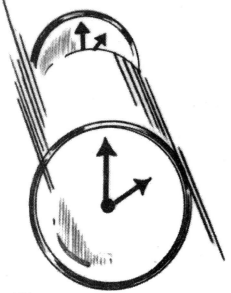

KEEP THINGS SIMPLE

On an outing, avoid confusing your child by calling attention to every new thing in sight. Instead, help him or her concentrate on three or four things that are of interest.

POINTING THINGS OUT

When you are pointing out something to your child, kneel down so that you are at his or her level. This allows you to help your child better understand what he or she is observing.

UP FRONT

When you are in a group with a tour guide, try standing in the front rather than in back. Children often are more quiet when they can really see and hear what is going on. Remind your child to "listen quietly to the person's story."

ENJOY IT ALL

Take time to enjoy with your child what may seem to you to be irrelevant. For instance, four flights of stairs in a row might be a wonderful mountain in your child's eyes. Fancy water fountains may require stops. Eating at a cafeteria or putting money in the parking meter might be the highlight of the outing. Having a positive experience together should be your goal.

WHEN YOU RETURN

WHAT DID WE DO?

Be sure to recall the outing with your child by reminding him or her about what you did. For a simple recall game, take turns repeating the sentence, "I saw a _____."

DRAMATIC PLAY

Set up play situations that encourage your child to reenact outings that you have taken. You'll find that your child enjoys using the information he or she has learned.

MAKING A DISPLAY

When you get back from an outing, display pictures and souvenirs of the trip and talk about them with your child. This will help keep the fun alive

PHOTO FUN

When your photos of an outing have been developed, let your child help put them into a special album. Encourage him or her to dictate captions for you to write under the photos.

KEEPING A JOURNAL

Keep a blank notebook, along with crayons and felt tip markers, in your car. Your child can draw pictures of your outings in it and dictate sentences for you to add. Later, photocopy the pages and send them to family members as letters, or use them to make a book for your child to "read."

FAMILY MEMBERSHIP

After visiting a place that you really enjoy, such as a museum or zoo, consider investing in a family membership. That way, you and your child can go often for short visits without feeling that you have to "get your money's worth" each time.

INDEX

Totline Teaching Tales are stories for sharing!

The front part of these children's books contains a wonderful tale that is delightfully illustrated in full color. The back of each book expands upon the themes of the story with related activity ideas: songs, poems, recipes, art, and movement!

Children ages 2 to 5 will enjoy the books as "read-alouds."

Children ages 6 to 8 can use the books as "easy-readers" and will be able to follow the simple instructions for the activities mostly on their own.

Kids Celebrate the Alphabet

Themes: Letters, Occupations
Jean Warren's newest children's story is told in rhyming verse. The beautiful, antibias art captivates children as well as adults. Encourage children to find the occupations featured on each page. Related activity pages follow the story. 32 pp.
Paperback WPH 1931

NATURE SERIES

These wonderful stories by Jean Warren focus on unique environments in nature. Filled with captivating illustrations, each story lets nature tell a gentle lesson. Related activities and songs ensure hours of fun. Each 32 pp.

Ellie the Evergreen

Themes: Fall, Winter, Self-Esteem
When the trees in the park turn beautiful colors in the fall, Ellie the Evergreen feels left out—until something special happens to her too.
Paperback WPH 1901 • Hardback WPH 1902

The Wishing Fish

Themes: Trees, North & South, Hot & Cold
A palm tree and a fir tree each get their wish to move to a different climate—thanks to the magical powers of the rainbow Wishing Fish.
Paperback WPH 1903 • Hardback WPH 1904

The Bear and the Mountain

Themes: Bears, Flowers, Friendship
Feel the joy of friendship as a playful bear cub and a lonely mountain get to know each other through the seasons of the year.
Paperback WPH 1905 • Hardback WPH 1906

Great Resources for Parents!